# K Reading INSTRUCTION

W9-BJN-548

Project Managers: Diane Arnell, Martha Goodale, Claudia Herman, Maura Wolk
Cover Designer and Illustrator: Julia Bourque
Book Design: Mark Nodland

Director–Product Development: Daniel J. Smith
Vice President–Product Development: Adam Berkin

ISBN 978-0-7609-8714-8
©2014—Curriculum Associates, LLC
North Billerica, MA 01862

30 29 28 27 26 25 24 23 22

BTS18

807169

# Table of Contents

# Table of Contents

 Draw.

Have children draw a picture of Jamaica and Russell. Display illustrations on pages 5–7, 19, and 25 to help them recall what each character looks like.

**Turn Talk** Use your pictures and evidence from the story to tell your partner what you know about each character.

Draw.

Have children draw a picture that shows how Jamaica feels after Russell scribbles on her drawing. Reread pages 10–12 to help them recall the details.

**Turn Talk** *How do you know that Jamaica feels angry?* Answer this question with your partner, using evidence from the story.

Draw.

Have children draw a picture that shows how Jamaica feels when she thinks about moving. Reread pages 20–21 to help them recall the details.

**Turn Talk** *Why does Jamaica feel sad? Answer this question with your partner, using evidence from the story.*

✏️ **Draw.**

Have children draw a picture that shows what Jamaica does at the end of the story. Reread page 26 to help them recall the details.

**Turn Talk** *Why does Jamaica decide to give Russell her blue marker? Answer this question with your partner, using evidence from the story.*

 **Draw.**

Have children draw a picture of Tommy and Mrs. Bowers. Display illustrations on pages 3 and 26 to help them recall what each character looks like.

**Turn Talk** Use your pictures and evidence from the story to tell your partner what you know about each character.

✏️ **Draw.**

Have children draw a picture that shows what Tommy likes to do. Reread pages 3–5 to help them recall the details.

**Turn Talk** *Why does Tommy want to be an artist when he grows up? Answer this question with your partner, using evidence from the story.*

✏️ Draw.

Have children draw a picture that shows how Tommy feels when Miss Landers tells him that he can't use his new crayons. Reread pages 22–23 to help them recall the details.

**Turn Talk** *Why does Tommy feel upset about not using his own crayons? Answer this question with your partner, using evidence from the story.*

**Draw.**

Have children draw a picture that shows what Tommy draws to be fair to the class. Reread pages 28–30 to help them recall the details.

**Turn Talk** *Why does Tommy draw two pictures?* Answer this question with your partner, using evidence from the story.

✏️ **Draw.**

Have children draw a picture of Chrysanthemum and Victoria. Display illustrations on pages 8, 11, and 19 to help them recall what each character looks like.

**Turn Talk** Use your pictures and evidence from the story to tell your partner what you know about each character.

✏ **Draw.**

Have children draw a picture that shows how Chrysanthemum feels about her name at the beginning of the story. Reread pages 5–7 to help them recall the details.

**Turn Talk** *Why does Chrysanthemum think her name is perfect? Answer this question with your partner, using evidence from the story.*

✏️ Draw.

Have children draw a picture that shows what happens when Chrysanthemum goes to school. Reread pages 9–10 to help them recall the details.

**Turn Talk** *Why do the girls make fun of Chrysanthemum's name? Answer this question with your partner, using evidence from the story.*

**Draw.**

Have children draw a picture that shows who helps Chrysanthemum feel happy about her name again. Reread pages 27–29 to help them recall the details.

**Turn Talk** *Why does Chrysanthemum feel happy about her name again?* Answer this question with your partner, using evidence from the story.

 Draw.

Have children draw a picture of the three soldiers and some peasants. Display illustrations on pages 16–17 to help them recall what the characters look like.

**Turn Talk** Use your pictures and evidence from the story to tell your partner what you know about each character.

# In the Beginning

✎ **Draw.**

Have children draw a picture that shows what the peasants do when they see the soldiers coming to their village. Reread pages 10–11 to help them recall the details.

**Turn Talk** *Why do the peasants hide their food when the soldiers come?* Answer this question with your partner, using evidence from the story.

# In the Middle

✏ **Draw.**

Have children draw a picture that shows some of the foods the peasants bring to add to the stone soup. Reread pages 26–33 to help them recall the details.

**Turn Talk** *Why do the peasants help the soldiers make stone soup?* Answer this question with your partner, using evidence from the story.

✏ **Draw.**

Have children draw a picture that shows what the peasants and the soldiers do when the stone soup is ready. Reread pages 36–37 to help them recall the details.

**Turn Talk** *How did the soldiers solve their problem of being hungry?* Answer this question with your partner, using evidence from the story.

Draw.

Have children draw a picture of the mosquito and Mother Owl. Display illustrations on pages 6, 12, and 27 to help them recall what each character looks like.

**Turn Talk** Use your pictures and evidence from the story to tell your partner what you know about each character.

✎ Draw.

Have children draw a picture that shows what Mother Owl usually does to end the night and bring the morning. Reread pages 12–13 to help them recall the details.

**Turn Talk** *Why doesn't Mother Owl wake up the sun?* Answer this question with your partner, using evidence from the story.

✎ **Draw.**

Have children draw a picture that shows what the animals do together in this part of the story. Reread pages 14–15 to help them recall the details.

**Turn Talk** *What does King Lion want to find out?* Answer this question with your partner, using evidence from the story.

✏️ **Draw.**

Have children draw a picture that shows why the other animals cannot find the mosquito. Reread page 30 to help them recall the details.

**Turn Talk** *Why do mosquitoes buzz in people's ears?* Answer this question with your partner, using evidence from the story.

 Circle.

 Draw.

Have children circle the picture that shows what the book *Red-Eyed Tree Frog* is mostly about. Point to and name each picture *(a red-eyed tree frog; an animal that lives in a shell; a swimmer; a fish)*. Then have children draw one important thing they learned from the book. For example, they might draw what a red-eyed tree frog will not eat.

**Turn Talk** Tell your partner one important thing you learned from this book. Use your picture and evidence from the book to support your ideas.

✏ Draw.

Have children draw a picture that shows what the red-eyed tree frog does during the day. Reread page 5 to help them recall the details.

**Turn Talk** *When does the red-eyed tree frog wake up? What does it do when it is awake?* Answer these questions with your partner, using evidence from the book.

# Red-Eyed Tree Frog
# Staying Safe

✏️ Draw.

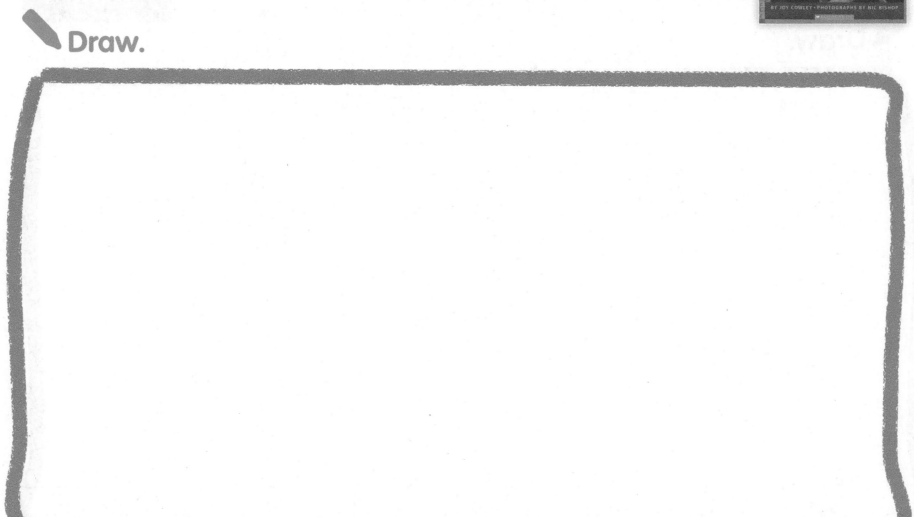

Have children draw a picture that shows how a red-eyed tree frog gets away from a hungry animal. Reread pages 16–19 to help them recall the details.

**Turn Talk** *How do you know the boa snake wants to eat the red-eyed tree frog? Answer this question with your partner, using evidence from the book.*

✏️ Draw.

Have children draw a picture that shows something a red-eyed tree frog will eat. Reread pages 21–23 to help them recall the details.

**Turn Talk** *What does a red-eyed tree frog do during the night? Answer this question with your partner, using evidence from the book.*

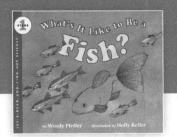

**Circle.**

**Draw.**

Have children circle the picture that shows what the book *What's It Like to Be a Fish?* is mostly about. Point to and name each picture *(a red-eyed tree frog; an animal that lives in a shell; a swimmer; a fish)*. Then have children draw one important thing they learned from the book. For example, they might draw a fish that has scales.

**Turn Talk** Tell your partner one important thing you learned from this book. Use your picture and evidence from the book to support your ideas.

# A Fish's Body

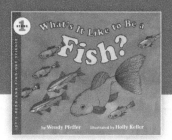

 **Draw.**

Have children draw a picture that shows a goldfish with five types of fins. Tell them to circle the fin that pushes the goldfish through the water. Reread pages 10–13 to help them recall the details.

**Turn Talk** *What parts of a fish's body help it to swim?* Answer this question with your partner, using evidence from the book.

# How Fish Breathe

✏️ Draw.

Have children draw a picture that shows a fish. Tell them to circle the part of the fish that opens and closes when the fish breathes. Reread pages 16–18 to help them recall the details.

**Turn Talk** *What parts of a fish's body does it use to breathe? How does a fish get oxygen? Answer these questions with your partner, using evidence from the book.*

✏️ **Draw.**

Have children draw a picture that shows a fish and something that the fish eats. Reread pages 20–23 to help them recall the details.

**Turn Talk** *What does a pet fish eat? What does a fish in the wild eat?* Answer these questions with your partner, using evidence from the book.

## Circle.

## Draw.

Have children circle the picture that shows what the book *What Lives in a Shell?* is mostly about. Point to and name each picture *(a red-eyed tree frog; an animal that lives in a shell; a swimmer; a fish)*. Then have children draw one important thing they learned from the book. For example, they might draw a snail hiding in its shell from a bird.

**Turn Talk** Tell your partner one important thing you learned from this book. Use your picture and evidence from the book to support your ideas.

# A Shell Is a Home

✏️ Draw.

Have children draw a picture that shows one home that is not a shell and one home that is a shell. Reread pages 5–8 to help them recall the details.

**Turn Talk** *Why are homes important to the people or animals that live in them?* Answer this question with your partner, using evidence from the book.

✏️ Draw.

Have children draw a picture that shows a snail that is taking its home with it as it moves. Reread pages 11–12 to help them recall the details.

**Turn Talk** *How does a snail move? Why doesn't it leave its home?* Answer these questions with your partner, using evidence from the book.

# A Shell That Fits

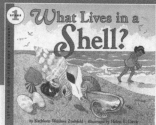

**Draw.**

Have children draw a picture that shows an animal whose shell fits it like a suit of armor. Reread pages 18–19 to help them recall the details.

**Turn Talk** *What does a crab do when it outgrows its shell?* Answer this question with your partner, using evidence from the book.

## Circle.

## Draw.

Have children circle the picture that shows what the book *America's Champion Swimmer* is mostly about. Point to and name each picture *(a red-eyed tree frog; an animal that lives in a shell; a swimmer; a fish)*. Then have children draw one important thing they learned from the book. For example, they might draw people greeting Trudy after she swims the English Channel.

**Turn Talk** Tell your partner one important thing you learned from this book. Use your picture and evidence from the book to support your ideas.

✏️ Draw.

Have children draw a picture that shows Trudy winning her first big swimming race. Reread page 8 to help them recall the details.

**Turn Talk** *What big swimming challenge does Trudy want to take on? Answer this question with your partner, using evidence from the book.*

# Swimming the Channel

✏ Draw.

Have children draw a picture that shows one thing that helps Trudy during her swim across the Channel. Reread pages 18–23 to help them recall the details.

**Turn Talk** *Why does Trudy get scared during her swim across the Channel? Answer this question with your partner, using evidence from the book.*

✎ **Draw.**

Have children draw a picture that shows the way Trudy celebrates in New York City. Reread pages 30–31 to help them recall the details.

**Turn Talk** *Why was Trudy's swim across the English Channel important to women all over the world?* Answer this question with your partner, using evidence from the book.

# Asking Questions

Asking questions helps you understand important information in a story.

When you are reading or listening to a story, you should ask questions. Begin each question with one of these words:

**Who**     **Where**     **What**

**When**     **Why**     **How**

Finding answers to your questions helps you understand the story.

 Circle.

 Circle.

 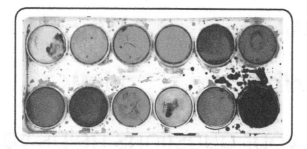 

Model completing the page. For the first item, ask: *What does Jack collect?* Point to and name each picture *(sand castles; turtles; drawings)*. Demonstrate circling the correct answer. Continue with the second item. Ask: *What does Tommy use to draw? (crayons; paint; markers)*

**Turn Talk** *What different things do Tommy and his friends like to do?* Ask and answer this question with your partner.

 Circle.

 Circle.

Guide children to complete the page. For the first item, ask: *Where are Jamaica and Russell?* Point to and name each picture *(at the playground; in the classroom; at home)*. Have a volunteer tell which picture to circle. Continue with the second item. Ask: *What does Jamaica share?* *(markers; construction paper; chalk)*

**Turn Talk** With your partner, ask and answer *what* questions about this part of the story. For example, ask: *What does Jamaica draw?*

*Jamaica's Blue Marker*

 Circle.

 Circle.

Have children complete the page independently. For the first item, ask: *What does Russell draw?* Point to and name each picture *(a tree; a piece of cake; squiggly circles)*. Have children circle their answers. Continue with the second item. Ask: *What does Russell use to draw? (paint; a blue marker; modeling clay)*

**Turn Talk** With your partner, ask and answer a question about this part of the story. Use *who, where,* or *what* to begin your question.

# Identifying Characters

A **character** is a person or an animal in a story.

When you are reading or listening to a story, ask:

- What do the characters say?
- What do the characters do?
- How do the characters feel?

Asking questions about characters helps you understand the story.

 Circle.

 Circle.

Model completing the page. For the first item, ask: *Who is this story mostly about?*
Point to and name each picture *(a girl; a boy; a baby)*. Demonstrate circling the correct answer.
Continue with the second item. Ask: *What does Tommy want to be when he grows up?*
*(a baker; an artist; a baseball player)*

**Turn Talk** *What does Tommy do to show he wants to be an artist?*
Ask and answer this question with your partner.

# Practice Together
# Identifying Characters

 Circle.

 Circle.

---

Guide children to complete the page. For the first item, ask: *Who is the character in this story?* Point to and name each picture (*a mouse; an elephant; a penguin*). Have a volunteer tell which picture to circle. Continue with the second item. Ask: *How does Chrysanthemum feel about her name in this part of the story? (sad; surprised; happy)*

**Turn Talk** With your partner, ask and answer a question about Chrysanthemum. For example, ask: *What does Chrysanthemum do to show how she feels about her name?*

 Circle.

 Circle.

Have children complete the page independently. For the first item, ask: *What is Chrysanthemum named after?* Point to and name each picture *(a dress; a flower; sneakers).* Have children circle their answers. Continue with the second item. Ask: *How does Chrysanthemum feel about her name in this part of the story? (happy; sad; surprised)*

**Turn Talk** *How does Victoria feel about Chrysanthemum's name? What does Victoria say that makes you think that?* Ask and answer these questions with your partner.

# Identifying Setting

The **setting** is when and where a story takes place.

When you are reading or listening to a story, ask:

- When does the story take place?
- Where does the story take place?

Thinking about the setting helps you understand the story.

 Circle.

 Draw.

Model completing the page. For the first item, ask: *When does this part of the story take place?* Point to and name each picture *(morning; evening; nighttime).* Demonstrate circling the correct answer. Continue with the second item. Ask: *Where does this part of the story take place?* Model drawing the setting. Have children draw in their own books.

**Turn Talk** *What clues show when this part of the story happens? What clues show where this part of the story happens?* Ask and answer these questions with your partner.

 Circle.

 Draw.

Guide children to complete the page. For the first item, ask: *When does this part of the story take place?* Point to and name each picture *(morning; evening; nighttime)*. Have a volunteer tell which picture to circle. Continue with the second item. Ask: *Where does this part of the story take place?* Have children draw the setting.

**Turn Talk** With your partner, ask and answer questions about the setting of the story. For example, ask: *What picture clues show where the soldiers are in this part of the story?*

 Circle.

 Draw.

Have children complete the page independently. For the first item, ask: *When does this part of the story take place?* Point to and name each picture *(morning; evening; nighttime).* Have children circle their answers. Continue with the second item. Ask: *Where does this part of the story take place?* Have children draw the setting.

**Turn Talk** With your partner, ask and answer questions about clues to the setting of the story.

# Identifying Events

An **event** is something that happens in a story. **Major events** are the most important events in a story.

When you are reading or listening to a story, ask:

- What happens in this part of the story?
- What is the major event in this part of the story?

Thinking about events helps you understand a story.

 Write.

Russell gets cards from the class.

Jamaica gives Russell her blue marker.

The class plays games and eats cake.

Model completing the page. Ask: *What is the major event in this part of the story?* Point to each picture and read aloud its caption. Demonstrate writing the letter M to identify the major event.

**Turn Talk** *What is the major event in this part of the story? How do you know it's an important event?* Ask and answer these questions with your partner.

©Curriculum Associates, LLC   Copying is not permitted.

 **Write.**

Lion asks Rabbit a question.

The iguana is at the waterhole.

The python looks for a hiding place.

Guide children to complete the page. Ask: *What is the major event in this part of the story?* Point to each picture and read aloud its caption. Have a volunteer tell where to write the letter M.

**Turn Talk** With a partner, tell the major event in this part of the story. Tell how you know it is an important event.

 **Write.**

Mother Owl wakes
up the sun.

The mosquito hides
in a bush.

King Lion calls
a meeting.

Have children complete the page independently. Ask: *What is the major event in this part of the story?* Point to each picture and read aloud its caption. Have children write the letter M beneath the major event.

**Turn Talk** With your partner, tell the major event in this part of the story. Tell how you know it is an important event.

# Retelling Stories

When you **retell** a story, you tell important events and key details in order.

When you are reading or listening to a story, ask:

- What happens at the beginning?
- What happens next?
- What happens at the end?

Retelling helps you remember important events and key details in a story.

 Number.

Chrysanthemum loves her name.

Chrysanthemum starts school.

Children laugh at Chrysanthemum's name.

Model completing the page. Ask: *Which event happens first in this part of the story?* Point to each picture and read its caption. Demonstrate writing the numeral 1. Continue with the remaining boxes. Ask: *Which event happens next? Which event happens last?*

**Turn Talk** *What happens in this part of the story?* Ask and answer this question with your partner.

✎ Number.

Children make fun of Chrysanthemum's name.

Chrysanthemum does not like her name.

Chrysanthemum's parents help her feel better.

Guide children to complete the page. Ask: *Which event happens first in this part of the story?* Point to each picture and read its caption. Have a volunteer tell where to write the numeral 1. Continue with the remaining events. Ask: *Which event happens next? Which event happens last?*

**Turn Talk** *What happens in this part of the story?* Ask and answer this question with your partner.

 Number.

Mrs. Twinkle likes Chrysanthemum's name.

_____

The girls all want flower names.

_____

Chrysanthemum likes her name again.

_____

Have children complete the page independently. Ask: _Which event happens first in this part of the story?_ Point to each picture and read its caption. Have children write the numeral 1. Continue with the remaining events. Ask: _Which event happens next? Which event happens last?_

**Turn Talk** _What happens in this part of the story?_ Ask and answer this question with your partner.

# Asking Questions

A **key detail** is an important piece of information. Asking questions helps you understand key details.

When you are reading or listening to an information book, you should ask questions. Begin each question with one of these words:

| | | |
|---|---|---|
| **Who** | **Where** | **What** |
| **When** | **Why** | **How** |

Finding answers to your questions helps you understand an information book.

# Asking Questions

 Circle.

  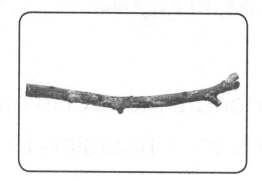  

 Circle.

Model completing the page. For the first item, ask: *Where is the red-eyed tree frog?* Point to and name each picture *(on a rock; on a branch; on a leaf)*. Demonstrate circling the correct answer. Continue with the second item. Ask: *What does the red-eyed tree frog eat? (ant; moth; katydid)*

**Turn Talk** *What animal does the frog eat? How do you know?* Ask and answer these questions with your partner.

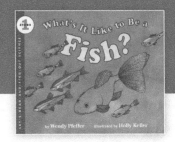

 Circle.

 Circle.

Guide children to complete the page. For the first item, ask: *Where can a pet goldfish live?* Point to and name each picture *(in a goldfish bowl; in a swimming pool; in the ocean).* Have a volunteer tell which picture to circle. Continue with the second item. Ask: *Where can a pet goldfish hide?* *(in water plants; in gravel; in a castle)* Guide children to circle two pictures.

**Turn** With your partner, ask and answer a *what* question about this part
**Talk** of the book. For example, ask: *What can you watch in a fish bowl?*

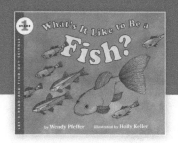

 Circle.

 Circle.

Have children complete the page independently. For the first item, ask: *Why are a fish's eyes always open?* Point to and name each picture *(fish have no eyelids; fish have eyelids; fish have no fins)*. Have children circle their answers. Continue with the second item. Ask: *How can you take care of a goldfish's eyes?* *(put fish in the sun; remove fish from the bowl; keep fish out of the sun)*

**Turn Talk** With your partner, ask and answer a question about this part of the book. Use *how* or *why* to begin your question.

# Main Topic

The **main topic** is what a book, or part of a book, is all about.

When you are reading or listening to an information book, ask:

- What is this book all about?
- What are the key details?

The main topic is what the key details are all about.

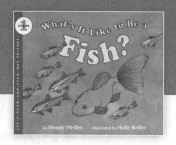

## Main Topic

 Circle.

Model completing the page. Read aloud the main topic: *A fish's body is perfect for swimming.* Then reread the second paragraph on page 10. Each time you read a key detail, pause to model circling the corresponding picture (*fish body; fish fins; fish tail*).

**Turn Talk** *What makes a fish a good swimmer?* Ask and answer this question with your partner.

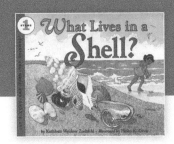

## Main Topic

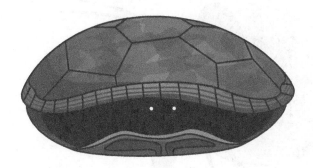

 Circle.

Guide children to complete the page. Read aloud page 17 and help children decide what all the key details are about. *(A turtle stays safe in a shell.)* Then as you reread page 17, guide children to circle the corresponding picture as you read a key detail. *(The turtle is afraid of the cat; the turtle cannot run fast; the turtle pulls its head, legs, and tail into its shell.)*

**Turn Talk** With your partner, retell key details that tell why a turtle hides in its shell. For example, say: *The turtle is afraid of the cat.*

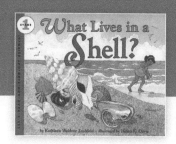

# Main Topic

 Circle.

Have children complete the page independently. Read aloud pages 22–23 and state the main topic: *A hermit crab lives in an empty snail shell.* Then, as you reread the pages, have children circle the corresponding picture as you read a key detail (*a hermit crab's body is soft; a hermit crab cannot stay safe from enemies; a hermit crab outgrows its shell*).

**Turn Talk** With your partner, tell the main topic of this part of the book. Retell the key details.

# Describing Connections

To **connect** means to fit together. Here are two kinds of connections:

In **time order**, one event follows another in order.

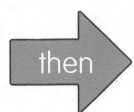 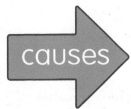 then

In **cause and effect**, one event causes another to happen.

 causes

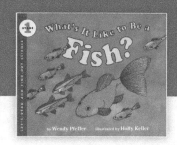

 Circle.

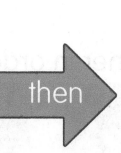

then

Time Order

Cause and Effect

Model completing the page. Point to and name each picture *(goldfish racing to the top; goldfish gulping down food)*. Model using the clue word *then* to describe the connection. Then ask: *How do you describe the connection when one event follows another one?* Model circling the correct answer.

**Turn Talk** *What word can you use to describe the connection between the events? Ask and answer this question with your partner.*

 Circle.

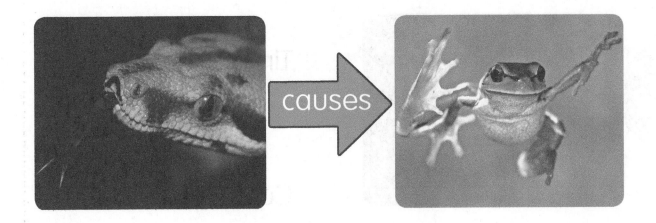

Time Order

Cause and Effect

Guide children to complete the page. Point to and name each picture *(snake flicking its tongue; frog jumping)*. Guide a volunteer to use the clue word *causes* to describe the connection. Then ask: *How do you describe the connection when one event causes another?* Read the answer choices, and guide children to circle the correct one.

**Turn Talk** With your partner, use the word *causes* to describe the connection between the events.

 Circle.

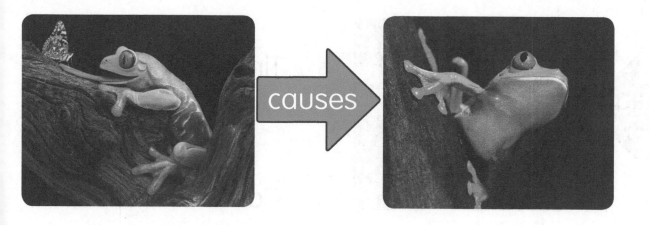

Time Order

Cause and Effect

Have children complete the page. Point to and name each picture *(frog eating a moth; frog is not hungry)*. Have a volunteer use the clue word *causes* to describe the connection. Then ask: *How do you describe the connection when one event causes another?* Read the answer choices, and have children circle the correct one.

**Turn Talk** With your partner, describe the connection between the events.

# Unknown Words

Sometimes you hear or read a word you do not know. You can ask questions about the word to find out what it means.

Here are some questions you can ask:

- What clues can I find in the other words?
- What clues can I find in the pictures?

Finding the meaning of new words can help you understand a story.

 **Circle.**

 **Circle.**

Model completing the page. For the first item, ask: *Which picture shows someone trudging?* Demonstrate circling the correct picture. Continue with the second item. Ask: *Which picture shows a village?* Discuss the evidence that helped you choose each correct picture.

**Turn Talk** With your partner, ask and answer questions about the word *trudged*. For example, ask: *What evidence in* Stone Soup *tells about the word* trudged?

# Practice Together
# Unknown Words

 Circle.

 Circle.

Guide children to complete the page. For the first item, ask: *Which picture shows a burrow?* Guide children to circle the correct picture. Continue with the second item. Ask: *Which picture shows someone scurrying?* Discuss the evidence that helped children choose each correct picture.

**Turn Talk** *What evidence in the story tells about the word* scurried? Ask and answer this question with your partner.

 Circle.

 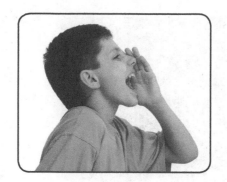 

 Circle.

Have children complete the page independently. For the first item, ask: *Which picture shows someone crying out?* Have children circle the correct picture. Continue with the second item. Ask: *Which picture shows a limb?* Have children discuss the evidence that helped them choose each correct picture.

**Turn Talk** With your partner, ask and answer questions about the words *crying* and *limb.*

# Types of Texts

A **text** is a piece of writing. Here are some different types of texts:

- A poem is a short text written in lines. Many poems have rhyming words.
- A story includes characters, a setting, and events. Most stories have pictures.
- A recipe tells you how to make something.

Knowing what type of text you are reading helps you understand more about it.

 **Circle.**

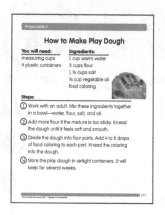  

 **Circle.**

Model completing the page. For the first item, ask: *What type of text is "The Owl and the Pussy-Cat"*? Point to and name each picture *(recipe; story; poem)*. Demonstrate circling the correct answer. Continue with the second item. Ask: *What type of text often has rhyming words? (recipe; story; poem)*

**Turn Talk** *How can you tell that "The Owl and the Pussy-Cat" is a poem?* Ask and answer this question with your partner.

STONE SOUP
by Marcia Brown

 Circle.

**How to Make Play Dough**

You will need:
measuring cups
4 plastic containers

Ingredients:
1 cup warm water
3 cups flour
1 ½ cups salt
¼ cup vegetable oil
food coloring

Steps:
1. Work with an adult. Mix these ingredients together in a bowl—water, flour, salt, and oil.
2. Add more flour if the mixture is too sticky. Knead the dough until it feels soft and smooth.
3. Divide the dough into four parts. Add 4 to 6 drops of food coloring to each part. Knead the coloring into the dough.
4. Store the play dough in airtight containers. It will keep for several weeks.

Three soldiers came to a village. They were very hungry.

No one wanted to feed them, so they decided to make stone soup.

**The Owl and the Pussy-Cat**
by Edward Lear,
*Nonsense Songs, Stories, Botany, and Alphabets*

I
The Owl and the Pussy-Cat went to sea
In a beautiful pea green boat:
They took some honey, and plenty of money
Wrapped up in a five-pound note.
The Owl looked up to the stars above,
And sang to a small guitar,
"O lovely Pussy! O Pussy my love,
What a beautiful Pussy you are,
You are,
You are!
What a beautiful Pussy you are!"

II
Pussy said to the Owl, "You elegant fowl,
How charmingly sweet you sing!
Oh! let us be married; too long we have tarried:

 Circle.

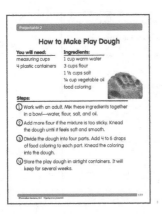

**How to Make Play Dough**

You will need:
measuring cups
4 plastic containers

Ingredients:
1 cup warm water
3 cups flour
1 ½ cups salt
¼ cup vegetable oil
food coloring

Steps:
1. Work with an adult. Mix these ingredients together in a bowl—water, flour, salt, and oil.
2. Add more flour if the mixture is too sticky. Knead the dough until it feels soft and smooth.
3. Divide the dough into four parts. Add 4 to 6 drops of food coloring to each part. Knead the coloring into the dough.
4. Store the play dough in airtight containers. It will keep for several weeks.

Three soldiers came to a village. They were very hungry.

No one wanted to feed them, so they decided to make stone soup.

**The Owl and the Pussy-Cat**
by Edward Lear,
*Nonsense Songs, Stories, Botany, and Alphabets*

I
The Owl and the Pussy-Cat went to sea
In a beautiful pea green boat:
They took some honey, and plenty of money
Wrapped up in a five-pound note.
The Owl looked up to the stars above,
And sang to a small guitar,
"O lovely Pussy! O Pussy my love,
What a beautiful Pussy you are,
You are,
You are!
What a beautiful Pussy you are!"

II
Pussy said to the Owl, "You elegant fowl,
How charmingly sweet you sing!
Oh! let us be married; too long we have tarried:

Guide children to complete the page. For the first item, ask: *What type of text is* Stone Soup? Point to and name each picture *(recipe; story; poem)*. Have a volunteer tell which picture to circle. Continue with the second item. Ask: *What type of text has characters, a setting, and events? (recipe; story; poem)*

**Turn Talk** Tell your partner how you know what type of text *Stone Soup* is. For example, say: Stone Soup *has characters—the soldiers and the peasants.*

## How to Make
## Play Dough

 **Circle.**

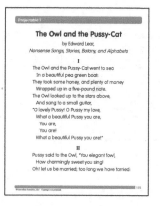

 **Circle.**

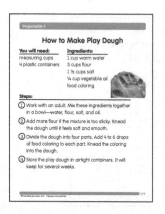

Have children complete the page independently. For the first item, ask: *What type of text is "How to Make Play Dough"?* Point to and name each picture *(recipe; story; poem)*. Have children circle their answer. Continue with the second item. Ask: *What type of text tells how to make something? (recipe; story; poem)*

**Turn Talk** Tell your partner how you know what type of text "How to Make Play Dough" is.

# Authors and Illustrators

An author and illustrator work together to tell a story.

- The **author** writes the words.
- The **illustrator** draws the pictures that go with the words.

Before you read or listen to a story, ask:

- Who is the author?
- Who is the illustrator?

You will know who tells the story.

 **Match.**

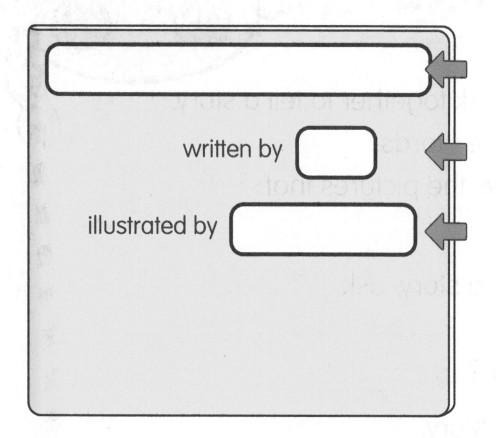

written by

illustrated by

Jamaica's Blue Marker

Juanita Havill

Anne Sibley O'Brien

Model completing the page. Point to and read aloud the words on the book cover. Then point to each blank box and tell what words go in the box *(story title; name of the author; name of the illustrator)*. Read aloud the answer choices. Model drawing a line from each answer choice to its place on the book cover.

**Turn Talk** *What did the illustrator draw for the cover picture? Ask and answer this question with your partner.*

 **Match.**

Why Mosquitoes Buzz
in People's Ears

written by          illustrated by

Verna Aardema

Leo and Diane Dillon

Guide children to complete the page. Point to and read aloud the words on the book cover. Then point to each blank box and have volunteers tell what words go in the box *(story title; name of the author; name of the illustrator)*. Read aloud the answer choices. Have children draw a line from each answer choice to its place on the book cover.

**Turn Talk** With your partner, ask and answer a question about the author or illustrators of this story. For example, ask: *Who illustrated this story?*

 **Match.**

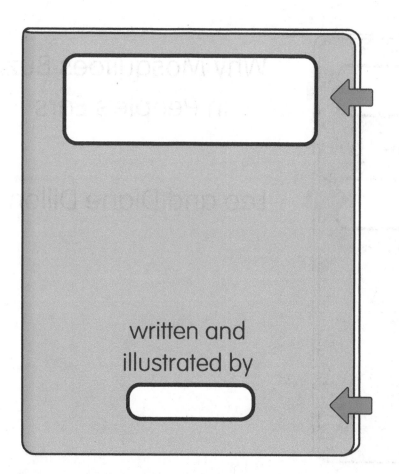

written and
illustrated by

The Art Lesson

Tomie dePaola

Have children complete the page independently. Point to and read aloud the words on the book cover. Have volunteers tell what words go in each blank box *(story title; name of the author-illustrator)*. Then read aloud the answer choices. Have children draw a line from each answer choice to its place on the book cover.

**Turn Talk** *Why do you think the author chose this title for the story?* Ask and answer this question with your partner.

# Unknown Words

Sometimes you hear or read a word you do not know. You can ask questions about the word to find out what it means.

Here are some questions you can ask:

- What clues can I find in the other words?
- What clues can I find in the pictures?

Finding the meaning of new words can help you understand an information book.

 Circle.

 Circle.

Model completing the page. For the first item, ask: *Which picture shows a trainer?* Demonstrate circling the correct picture. Continue with the second item. Ask: *Which picture shows a shore?* Discuss the evidence that helped you choose each correct picture.

**Turn Talk** *What evidence in the book tells about the word* shore? Ask and answer this question with your partner.

# Practice Together
## Unknown Words

 Circle.

 Circle.

Guide children to complete the page. For the first item, ask: *Which picture shows a katydid?* Guide children to circle the correct picture. Continue with the second item. Ask: *Which picture shows how someone might feel after eating something poisonous?* Discuss the clues that helped children choose each correct picture.

**Turn Talk** With your partner, ask and answer questions about the word *poisonous*. For example, ask: *What clues in the book tell about the word* poisonous?

# Practice by Myself
## Unknown Words

 **Circle.**

 **Circle.**

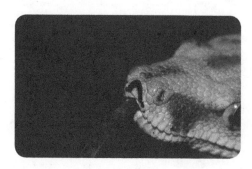

Have children complete the page independently. For the first item, ask: *Which picture shows how an animal slithers?* Have children circle the correct picture. Continue with the second item. Ask: *Which picture shows how a snake flicks its tongue?* Have children discuss the clues that helped them choose each correct picture.

**Turn Talk** With your partner, ask and answer questions about the words *slither* and *flicks*.

# Parts of a Book

A book has different parts. Each part tells you something about the book.

Before you read or listen to a story, ask:
- What information is on the front cover?
- What information is on the title page?
- What information is on the back cover?

You can find out about a book by asking and answering these questions.

 **Circle.**

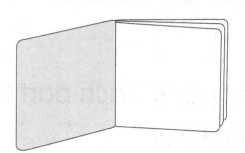

 **Circle.**

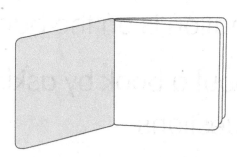

Model completing the page. For the first item, display the front cover of *Red-Eyed Tree Frog*. Ask: *What part of the book is this?* Point to and name each picture *(front cover; title page; back cover)*. Demonstrate circling the correct answer. Continue with the second item. Display the title page. Ask: *What part of the book is this? (front cover; title page; back cover)*

**Turn Talk** *Which parts of a book show the book's title?* Ask and answer this question with your partner.

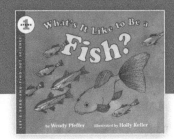

 Circle.

 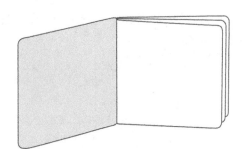 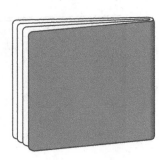

 Circle.

 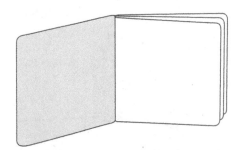 

Guide children to complete the page. For the first item, display the back cover of *What's It Like to Be a Fish?* Ask: *What part of the book is this?* Point to and name each picture *(front cover; title page; back cover)*. Have a volunteer tell which picture to circle. Continue with the second item. Display the front cover. Ask: *What part of the book is this? (front cover; title page; back cover)*

**Turn Talk** With your partner, tell what information you can find on the front cover of this book. For example, say: *The author is Wendy Pfeffer.*

 **Circle.**

    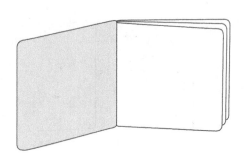    

 **Circle.**

    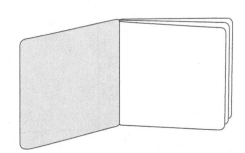    

Have children complete the page independently. For the first item, display the title page of *What Lives in a Shell?* Ask: *What part of the book is this?* Point to and name each picture *(front cover; title page; back cover).* Have children circle their answers. Continue with the second item. Display the front cover. Ask: *What part of the book is this? (front cover; title page; back cover)*

**Turn Talk** With your partner, name the parts of a book. Tell what information you can find written on each part.

# Story Words and Pictures

Stories usually have words and pictures that go together.

When you are reading or listening to a story, ask:

- What happens?
- What do the words tell about?
- What do the pictures show?

Words and pictures work together to tell what happens in a story.

 **Circle.**

| 1. | 2. | 3. |
|---|---|---|
| King Lion talks to the monkey. | A tree limb falls on the nest. | The crow calls and calls. |

Model completing the page. Ask children to look closely at the picture. Then read aloud the three sentences. Ask: *Which sentence tells what is happening in the picture?* Demonstrate circling the correct answer. Point to the picture again and reread the sentence that tells what is happening in the picture.

**Turn Talk** *What moment in* Why Mosquitoes Buzz in People's Ears *does the picture show?* Ask and answer this question with your partner.

 Circle.

1.

| The soldiers are cooking. |

2.

| Peasants hide sacks of barley. |

3.

| The peasant hides cabbages. |

Guide children to complete the page. Ask them to look closely at the picture. Then read aloud the three sentences. Ask: *Which sentence tells what is happening in the picture?* Have a volunteer tell which sentence to circle. Point to the picture again and reread the sentence that tells what is happening in the picture.

**Turn Talk** *What moment in* Stone Soup *does the picture show?* Ask and answer this question with your partner.

 Circle.

**1.** The soldiers stir the soup.

**2.** Children run to get salt.

**3.** A woman brings carrots.

Have children complete the page independently. Ask them to look closely at the picture. Then read aloud the three sentences. Ask: *Which sentence tells what is happening in the picture?* Have children circle their answers.

**Turn Talk** With your partner, tell what moment in *Stone Soup* the picture shows.

# Comparing Characters

You **compare** characters by telling how they are the same.

You **contrast** characters by telling how they are different.

When you are reading or listening to a story, ask:

- What do the characters do? Do they do the same things or different things?
- What do the characters say? Do they say the same things or different things?
- How do the characters feel? Do they feel the same way or different ways?

Jamaica's Blue Marker
Juanita Havill
Illustrations by Anne Sibley O'Brien

 **Circle.**

 **Circle.**

Model completing the page. For the first item, ask: *How does Russell feel about moving away?* Point to and describe each picture *(surprised; happy; sad)*. Demonstrate circling the correct answer. Continue with the second item. Ask: *In this part of the story, how does Jamaica feel about Russell moving away? (surprised; happy; sad)*

**Turn Talk** *Are Russell's and Jamaica's feelings the same or different?* Ask and answer this question with your partner.

 Circle.

 Circle.

Guide children to complete the page. For the first item, ask: *How does Chrysanthemum feel about her name?* Point to and describe each picture *(she loves it; she thinks it is funny; it makes her sad)*. Have a volunteer tell which picture to circle. Continue with the second item. Ask: *How do Chrysanthemum's classmates feel about her name?* *(they love it; they think it is funny; it makes them sad)*

**Turn Talk** With your partner, talk about how Chrysanthemum feels about her name. Then talk about how her classmates feel about her name. For example, say: *Chrysanthemum loves her name, but her classmates think her name is funny.*

 Circle.

 Circle.

Have children complete the page independently. For the first item, ask: *What is Chrysanthemum named after?* Point to and describe each picture *(a flower; her grandmother; a character in a story).* Have children circle their answers. Continue with the second item. Ask: *What is Mrs. Twinkle named after? (a flower; her grandmother; a character in a story)*

**Turn Talk** With your partner, tell what is the same about Mrs. Twinkle and Chrysanthemum. Then tell what is different.

# Words and Pictures

Words and pictures give information about the following:

**people**          **places**          **things**

**events**          **ideas**

When you are reading or listening to an information book, ask:

- What information do I get from the words?
- What information do I get from the pictures?
- How are the words and pictures connected?

Words and pictures work together to give information about a topic.

 Circle.

 Circle.

Model completing the page. For the first item, ask: *What information do you get from the words?* Point to and name each picture *(a crab; a girl at the beach; seashells)*. Demonstrate circling two correct answers. Continue with the second item. Ask: *What information do you get from the pictures? (a crab; a girl at the beach; seashells)*

**Turn Talk** *How are the words and the picture connected?* Ask and answer this question with your partner.

 Circle.

 Circle.

Guide children to complete the page. For the first item, ask: *What information do you get from the words?* Point to and name each picture *(a rowboat; a bathing cap and goggles; a bathing suit)*. Have volunteers tell which pictures to circle. Continue with the second item. Ask: *What information do you get from the pictures? (a rowboat; a bathing cap and goggles; a bathing suit)*

**Turn Talk** With your partner, tell what information you get from both the words and the picture. For example: *Trudy wore a bathing suit, bathing cap, and goggles.*

# Practice by Myself
# Words and Pictures

 Circle.

 Circle.

Have children complete the page independently. For the first item, ask: *What information do you get from the words?* Point to and name each picture *(a tugboat; choppy water; an arrow)*. Have children circle their answers. Continue with the second item. Ask: *What information do you get from the pictures? (a tugboat; choppy water; an arrow)*

**Turn Talk** With your partner, tell how the words and the picture in this part of the story are connected.

# Identifying Reasons

Authors have important ideas they want you to understand. They give **reasons** to explain their ideas.

When you are reading or listening to an information book, ask:

- What important idea does the author want me to know?
- What reason does the author give to explain why the idea is important?

Finding reasons helps you understand the author's ideas.

## Important Idea

 Circle.

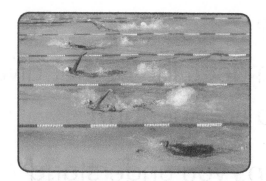

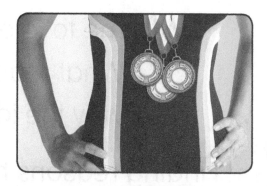

Model completing the page. Read aloud the important idea: *Gertrude Ederle's place was in the water.* Explain that children will circle each reason that explains this idea. Point to each picture and name the reason (*she loved to swim; she won a race at age fifteen; she won three Olympic medals*). Model deciding whether each reason explains the important idea, and circle the pictures. Revisit the text as needed.

**Turn Talk** *What did Gertrude Ederle do in the water?* Ask and answer this question with your partner.

# Identifying Reasons

Eat Better!

## Important Idea

 **Circle.**

Guide children to complete the page. Read aloud the important idea: *Fill your plate with fruits and vegetables.* Point to each picture and name the reason *(you will get vitamins and minerals to grow; you will have energy to play; you will feel better).* Help children decide whether each reason explains the important idea. Have them circle each reason that does.

**Turn Talk** With your partner, tell one reason why you should fill your plate with fruit and vegetables. For example, say: *Fruits and vegetables give you energy to play.*

## Important Idea

 Circle.

Have children complete the page independently. Read aloud the important idea: *Don't eat these types of food every day.* Point to each picture and name the reason *(they are high in fat; they have lots of salt; they have too much sugar).* Have children decide whether each reason explains the important idea. Have them circle each reason that does.

**Turn Talk** With your partner, talk about why you should not eat "sometimes" foods every day.

# Comparing Two Books

When you **compare** two books, you tell how they are the same. When you **contrast** two books, you tell how they are different.

When you are reading or listening to information books on the same topic, ask:

- What is the same about the pictures?
- What is different about the pictures?
- What is the same about the words?
- What is different about the words?

 **Circle.**

 **Circle.**

Model completing the page. For the first item, ask: *Where do fish live?* Point to and describe each picture *(in water; in a nest; in a shell)*. Demonstrate circling the correct picture. Continue with the second item. Ask: *Where do land snails live? (in water; in a nest; in a shell)*

**Turn Talk** *How is a fish's home different from a snail's home?* Ask and answer this question with your partner.

 Circle.

 Circle.

      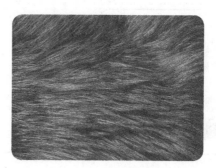

Guide children to complete the page. For the first item, ask: *What part of a fish's body helps to protect it?* Point to and describe each picture *(shell; scales; fur)*. Have a volunteer tell which picture to circle. Continue with the second item. Ask: *What part of a snail's body helps to protect it? (shell; scales; fur)*

**Turn Talk** With your partner, tell how the fish's body and the snail's body are different. For example, say: *A fish's body has scales, but a snail's body has a shell.*

# Practice by Myself
# Comparing Two Books

 **Circle.**

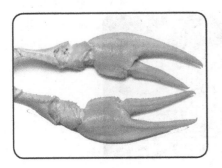  

 **Circle.**

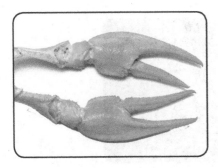  

Have children complete the page independently. For the first item, ask: *What do fish use to swim?* Point to and describe each picture *(claws; shell; tail)*. Have children circle their answers. Continue with the second item. Ask: *What do scallops use to swim? (claws; shell; tail)*

**Turn Talk** With a partner, tell what is different about how fish and scallops swim. Then tell what is the same about fish and scallops.